T0086102

Let's Make a

Battery

by Katie Chanez

NORWOOD HOUSE 🏠 PRESS

Norwood House Press

For information regarding Norwood House Press, please visit our website at:
www.norwoodhousepress.com or call 866-565-2900.

Hardcover ISBN: 978-1-68450-843-3
Paperback ISBN: 978-1-68404-619-5

LIBRARY OF CONGRESS CATALOGING-IN-PUBLICATION DATA

Names: Chanez, Katie, author.
Title: Let's make a battery / Katie Chanez.
Description: Chicago : Norwood House Press, 2021. | Series: Make your own: science experiment! | Includes bibliographical
    references and index. | Audience: Grades 2-3.
Identifiers: LCCN 2019058389 (print) | LCCN 2019058390 (ebook) | ISBN 9781684508433 (hardcover) | ISBN 9781684046195
    (paperback) | ISBN 9781684046256 (pdf)
Subjects: LCSH: Electric batteries--Juvenile literature. | Storage batteries--Juvenile literature. | Electricity--Juvenile literature. |
    Science--Experiments--Juvenile literature.
Classification: LCC TK2901 .C43 2020 (print) | LCC TK2901 (ebook) | DDC 621.31/242--dc23
LC record available at https://lccn.loc.gov/2019058389
LC ebook record available at https://lccn.loc.gov/2019058390

328N—072020
Manufactured in the United States of America in North Mankato, Minnesota.

Contents

CHAPTER 1

The replaceable batteries that commonly power devices come in many sizes.

All about Batteries

Batteries are everywhere. They power cell phones, laptops, cars, and more. Batteries store electricity so devices do not need to be plugged in. But batteries do run out of power over time. The first battery was invented in 1800. It was invented by Italian scientist Alessandro Volta. He believed he could use two different metals to create electricity. Volta layered metal discs between pieces of paper. Then he soaked the paper in salt water. This caused a

chemical reaction that created electricity. His battery worked! You will make your own battery with common ingredients too.

Batteries work because of the way **atoms** behave. Everything is made of atoms. Each atom has three types of **particles**. **Protons** and **neutrons** form the center of the atom. **Electrons** fly around the center. Protons have a positive charge. Electrons have a negative charge. And neutrons have no charge. Positive and negative charges pull together. Electrons are pulled like a magnet toward protons. This keeps the electrons close to the atom's center.

Not all electrons are equally drawn to the atom's center. The center pulls hardest on the electrons that are the closest. Sometimes electrons can be pulled to a different atom. Atoms have no charge

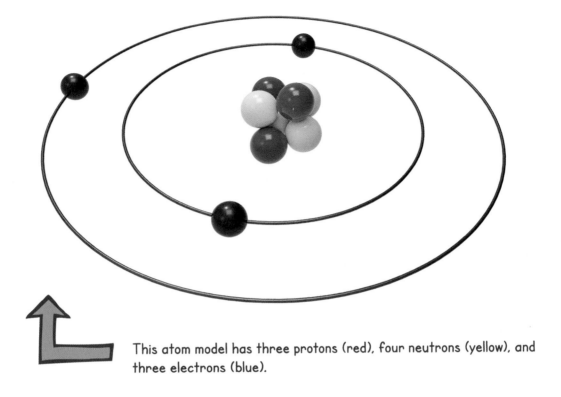

This atom model has three protons (red), four neutrons (yellow), and three electrons (blue).

when they have an equal number of protons and electrons. Atoms get a positive charge when electrons leave. Atoms get a negative charge when they gain electrons. Electricity is created by the movement of electrons.

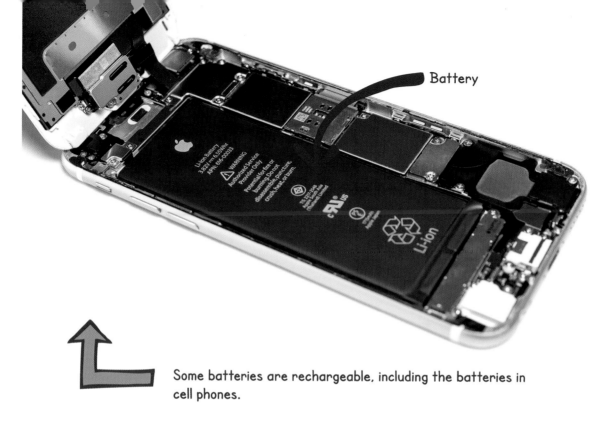

Battery

Some batteries are rechargeable, including the batteries in cell phones.

Batteries move electrons with chemical reactions. These reactions happen over a period of time. Batteries can last as little as a few hours and as long as several years.

A battery needs three parts for its chemical reactions. It has two **electrodes** and an **electrolyte**. The electrodes react with the electrolyte to create electricity. The electrodes allow electricity to flow into or out of the electrolyte. The electrolyte goes between the electrodes. The electrolyte allows electricity to flow through it.

Each electrode is made of a different kind of metal. Some metals lose electrons easily. Other metals gain electrons easily. A battery needs one electrode made of each type. This helps the electrons move. One electrode has a positive charge. It is in the center of the battery. The second one surrounds the positive electrode. It has a negative charge. The electrolyte is between them. The electrolyte can be a powder, liquid, or gel. Your battery will use a liquid electrolyte.

Batteries use two chemical reactions to work. The first happens at the negative electrode. Atoms from the negative electrode combine with atoms in the electrolyte. This process causes the atoms from the negative electrode to let go of electrons.

The electrons are pulled toward the positive end. But they cannot travel through the electrolyte. They need a different way to the other end of the battery. Wires can be used to connect the negative and positive ends. Then the electrons travel out of the negative end of the battery. They move through the wires.

The wires bring the electrons back to the positive end. This is where the second reaction happens. The positive electrode's atoms combine with the electrolyte's atoms. This creates new chemicals in

Most toys that light up or move need batteries to run.

the electrolyte. The negative electrode keeps reacting with the atoms in the electrolyte. The process continues to repeat.

The reactions do not begin until a path connects one end of the battery to the other. Wires create a path for the electrons to follow. This path is called a **circuit**. Electrons cannot travel without a complete circuit.

A device that uses the battery's power is called the **load**. The load is attached to the circuit. Turning the device on completes the circuit. The electrons travel out of the battery along wires. The wires lead them through the load. This powers the device. The electrons travel out of the load and back into the battery. Turning the device off breaks the circuit.

You can see this with a flashlight. Flipping the switch on connects the circuit. The electrons have a path to travel. The light bulb lights up. The light bulb is the load. Turning the flashlight off breaks the circuit. Then the light goes out.

Parts of a Battery

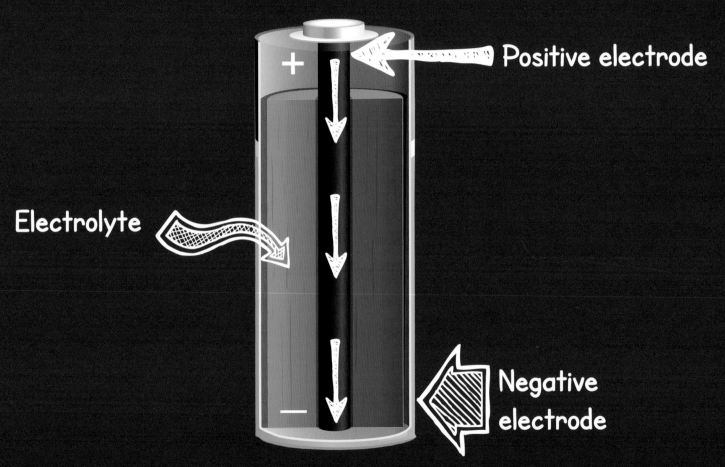

Positive electrode

Electrolyte

Negative electrode

Electron flow

Batteries are dangerous if they rust and allow the chemicals inside to be released.

CHAPTER 2

Make Your Own Battery

To make your battery, you need materials that will create electricity. Many batteries contain materials that are bad for the environment. These materials can also be unsafe for people. Most batteries have an outer metal case. This keeps the battery safe for people to use and touch. You will make a battery with safe materials. You will use common household items.

Not all materials allow electrons to travel through them. Those that do are called **conductors**. All of your materials need to conduct electricity. Your electrolyte will need to react with both electrodes. It must also conduct electricity. Lemons contain citric **acid**. This acid is what gives lemons their sour taste. It is also a good conductor. Citric acid reacts with metals. This makes lemon juice a good electrolyte.

Batteries use two different metals as electrodes. Your battery will too. One will be the negative electrode. It reacts with the lemon juice. This reaction lets electrons move out of the battery. Zinc is a common metal used in batteries. **Galvanized** nails have a zinc coating.

Lemon juice is one of the best natural sources of citric acid.

You will also need a positive electrode. Copper also reacts with lemon juice. The copper is positively charged. The reaction pulls the electrons back into the lemon. Copper wire has many uses. It is used in jewelry and art. It is also used inside wires to carry electricity.

A circuit forms when you put a battery in a device and turn it on. Electrons need a circuit in order to move. But you cannot put a lemon in a device. You will have to complete the circuit another way. Alligator clips are designed to connect wires. They will complete the circuit.

You need a way to see if your battery works. A light-emitting diode (LED) is a small bulb. It lights up when connected to a circuit. Your battery will not create a lot of power. But an LED does not need much. It will light up when connected to your battery.

Materials Checklist ⇨

✓ **Four lemons**

✓ **Copper wire**

✓ **Wire cutters**

✓ **Four galvanized nails**

✓ **Five alligator clips with wires**

✓ **One LED**

Do not break the peel when you roll or squeeze your lemons.

CHAPTER 3

Science Experiment!

Now that you know how batteries work, put your knowledge to use and make your own!

1. Roll the lemons on the table or gently squeeze them to soften them. This makes the juice flow inside the lemons.

2. Have an adult cut four small pieces of copper wire.

3. Push one piece of wire halfway into one end of each lemon.

23

4. Push a nail into the opposite end of each lemon. Make sure it does not touch the copper wire.

5. Connect one end of an alligator clip to a copper wire. Connect the other end to the nail in your second lemon.

26

6. Continue to connect your lemons with clips. Each piece of copper wire should be connected to a nail on another lemon. Your first and last lemon should each have one clip loose (one from a nail, one from a piece of copper wire).

7. Connect one loose clip to the LED.

8. Connect the other loose clip to the other end of the LED. If it does not light up, turn the LED around. The LED has positive and negative ends. You may have connected two positives and two negatives. Then, watch the electricity flow!

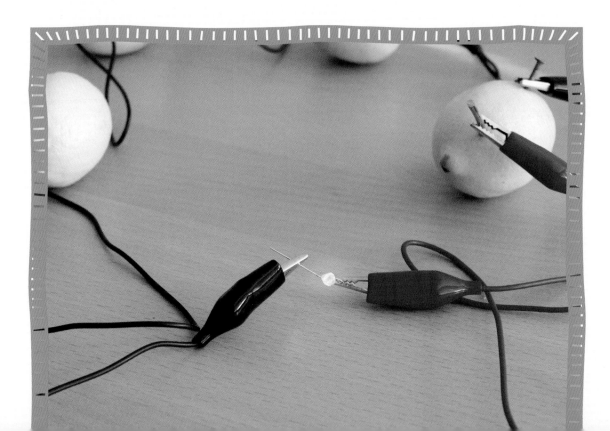

Make It Better!

Congratulations! You have made a battery. Now see if there are ways to improve it. Use any of these changes and see how they improve your battery.

- You used lemons to create your current. Are there other foods you could use? How do they affect the flow of electricity?

- You used copper wire as one of your electrodes. Copper can be found in many places. Pennies are covered in a copper coating. How is your battery affected when you change your copper source?

Can you think of any ways that you could improve or change your battery to make it better?

Glossary

acid **(A-sid):** A chemical that breaks down metals and tastes sour.

atoms **(AT-uhmz):** The basic pieces of matter that make up everything.

chemical reaction **(KEM-uh-kuhl ree-AK-shuhn):** A process in which the atoms in ingredients rearrange into something else.

circuit **(SIR-cut):** A path for electricity to follow.

conductors **(cuhn-DUHK-turz):** Materials that allow electricity to travel through them.

electrodes **(i-LEK-trohdz):** Conductors that allow electrons to pass in and out of an electrolyte.

electrolyte **(i-LEK-troh-lyt):** A chemical that reacts with the electrodes to create electricity.

electrons **(i-LEK-tronz):** Particles in an atom that travel around the nucleus and have a negative charge.

galvanized **(GAL-vuh-nyzd):** Covered in a zinc coating.

load **(LOHD):** The part of a circuit that uses electricity.

neutrons **(NOO-tronz):** Particles in an atom's nucleus that have no charge.

particles **(PAR-tuh-kuhlz):** Tiny pieces or amounts of something.

protons **(PROH-tonz):** Particles in an atom's nucleus that have a positive charge.

For More Information

Books

Maya Bayden. *What Is Chemical Energy?* New York, NY: Britannica Educational Publishing, 2018. Readers are shown how atoms are used to create chemical energy.

Steffi Cavell-Clarke. *Electricity*. New York, NY: KidHaven Publishing, 2018. This book explains electricity using many everyday examples.

Victoria G. Christensen. *How Batteries Work*. Minneapolis, MN: Lerner Publications, 2017. This book explores how batteries work and their different uses.

Websites

DK Find Out: Electricity (https://www.dkfindout.com/us/science/electricity/) This website discusses how electricity is created and its different uses.

Fun Kids Live: How Do Batteries Work? (https://www.funkidslive.com/learn/techno-mum/how-do-batteries-work/#) This website explains how batteries work and store energy.

Save on Energy: How Batteries Work (https://www.saveonenergy.com/how-batteries-work/) This source explains how electrons move inside a battery and includes animated graphics.

Index

About the Author

Katie Chanez is a children's book writer and editor originally from Iowa. She enjoys writing fiction, playing with her cat, and petting friendly dogs. Katie now lives and works in Minnesota.